GOING DOWN SINGING

KEVIN W. BURKE

Copyright © Kevin W. Burke 2018
No part of this book may be used or performed without written consent from the author, if living, except for critical articles or reviews.

Burke, Kevin W.
ISBN: 978-0-9890092-8-7
Edited by Bill Moran
Proofread by Gary Lovely
Additional Edits and Notes from Ebony Stewart and Lisa Thyer
Cover and Interior Design by Allison Truj

Printed in Tennessee, USA

Write About Now Publishing
Houston, TX
www.writeaboutnowpoetry.com

Timber Mouse Publishing
Austin, TX
www.timbermouse.com

*Dedicated to the memory of Erik Petersen.
I hope this book is to someone
what your music was to me.*

Thank you for the sun
Thank you for the blinds
Thank you for the
crack in the blinds
Thank you for these eyes
for waking up
for yawns
stretches
creaks and
cracks

for first breaths

Thank you for firsts
Thank you for firsts
that disguise themselves so well as
beginnings after an end
Thank you for the ends
and what's left but rebar

Thank you for what's behind me

Thank you for what's in front of me

Thank you for jeans
for boots
for miles
        and
                miles
                        and smiles
Thank you for teeth
these tuning forks for forgiveness
Thank you for ears
forgetting the shape of tone deaf in my mouth and
the sound

of skin on my tongue

Thank you for my tongue

for voice

for taste
Thank you for food
Thank you for sharing
Thank you for friends
for family
for hands

Thank you for work
and
worry
and cops
and suits and force and
ravishment
and broken t
                        rust
and the bastards who made me what I am
the fans for my flames the sides for my thorns thank you
for weary

for better days

for a home

for pride in action and sweat

for smoothed knots cradled crepitus and holding on.

Thank you for pillows

for sheets
and comforters and their palms
for the crack
                    in the blinds

for the blinds

for night

for night

                    for sleep
                                        for the time until the sun

Thank you for not doing it when I could have

When I wanted to
When it filled the windshield

I still can

I still hear wanting it sometimes

but thank you for not

and instead

turning around

and being thankful for the sun

thank you
                          for the sun
thank you for
                the sun

thank you for the sun

Thank you for the sun

CONTENTS

AGAINST MY ENVIRONMENT	12
A WORD OF ADVICE TO DRUNK KEVIN	14
NINETEEN NINETY-SEVEN	15
THE BAND PLAYED WALTZING MATILDA	16
EVEN IF THEY DON'T WANT TO	20
KIRBY ELEMENTARY	21
DRINKING TOWN WITH A SPORTS PROBLEM	22
DORM ROOM, WINTER '05	24
JOLIET 29	27
WHEN ASKED WHY I LISTEN TO MUSIC WHERE "THEY SCREAM SO MUCH"	28
JUNIOR MINTS	30
GRADUATION	33
AUSTIN, TX	35
PLEASE PROVIDE YOUR EMPLOYMENT HISTORY	37
DAY TWO	39
A SINCERE TOAST	43
THE SHAME BANK	49
I SAID FUCK OFF I'LL TALK LATER	51
THESAURUS	53
UNHINGED	54

DROP (excerpt)	55
HUNTING FOR LOST TREASURE (WE WON'T FIND)	56
DRIVE	58
I CONVINCE MYSELF I DON'T BELIEVE IN GHOSTS SO I CAN GET SOME SLEEP	62
THE LAST POEM I'LL WRITE ABOUT THE MESS WE MADE	63
ON SMASHING A GUITAR	65
FOR SHANE FOR THE IRISH THAT KEEPS HIM STANDING AND THE IRISH IN ME	66
WHAT WE WORK	69
BtMI	70
THE MOMENT YOU'RE AT A PUNK SHOW (OR ANYWHERE REALLY) AND DON'T KNOW THE WORDS	74
EIGHT STRING LULLABY	75
AGAIN. LOUDER. LET THE NEIGHBORS COMPLAIN.	79
GREEN GILLS LEARN TO BREATHE	82
SIXTEEN PINTS LATER	83
I WILL SCREAM THIS 'TIL WE'RE ALL DEAD	88
WE SLEEP WELL TOGETHER	91
WHAT KEEPS US TOGETHER	92
WHAT ARE YOUR INTENTIONS	93
OPEN YOUR EARS AND BREATHE	96
MY FAVORITE SONG	98
FIRE ACADEMY TRANSLATIONS	100
THIS IS WHAT THE VOLUME KNOB IS FOR	101

Cue
"No Trespassing Waltz"
Johnny Hobo + the Freight Trains
(the Chaos Infiltration Squad Version)

And it's true that we've teenage fools...

AGAINST MY ENVIRONMENT

The summer of '06 was a mess.

Broken strings
abandoned library parking lots
empty bottles
hand rolled cigarettes
Olympic Star
and, "Don't tell my mom."

I had taught myself guitar in winter
and was writing music now
for the first time.

It was no more drumming
for bands that all found ways to fall apart
before ever playing a show.
I was at the wheel now
putting words to the pain
in my uncalloused fingertips

and the discomfort under the rest of my skin.

The first songs I learned to play
were from Phil Ochs, Johnny Cash, and the Riot Folk collective
among others.

I did what any other young idiot with a guitar does
punched out the same three to five chords
G D Em C
over and
over and
over and
punched out my vocal chords and embarrassed throat
over and
over and
over and

at a time when I didn't have a hold on anything
I death gripped the neck of my buzzing guitar
until my fingers were numb
                        to all the burn.

A WORD OF ADVICE TO DRUNK KEVIN

Oak Park Avenue
(I think we were on Oak Park Avenue)
was finger painted by the street lights.
It looked like watercolors
still wet
tilted sideways
all the paint running out the frame
of Casey's car window.

He probably shouldn't have been driving
but I couldn't say shit to the guy.

Fuck it.

I think it was the drunkest I'd ever been in Tinley.

I spit out into the sloppy colors dripping by and farted,

"Sorry I farted, man."
"It's okay. Just,
next time you spit out the window
roll it down first."

Next time you're looking for an escape

take aim first.

NINETEEN NINETY-SEVEN

The lightning comes
down the chimney and hits a
gas
line

shoves   the dry wall and bricks
                                          onto the couch
claws at the studs
sets fire under the skin
   sha
        kes the house to the bone.

The whole thing scares the shit out of the dog,
it's all over the neighbor's floor he runs to.

We are in Michigan.
Summer family trip with the Sullivans.

When we get back
and the rotted tissue of the family room is removed
the room debrided to the foundation
me, my sister, and other kids in the neighborhood
put on our rollerblades and sidewalk chalk
and skate
and fall over

laughing
on tragedy scratched to rainbow

making sure we are living
burning in the shell of a burned out box

I remember my mom sitting on the stairs
smiling
louder than thunder.

THE BAND PLAYED WALTZING MATILDA

Irish man is born
on the South Side of Chicago.
Irish man meets South Side Polish-German girl.
Irish man grows up,
buys her a ring,
they have two kids,
Irish man becomes Irish Dad.

Irish Dad, he fixes things around the house.
On an old paint splattered boom box
Irish Dad listens to Johnny B, Da Bears, and Steve Dahl on the radio
and an old cassette of even older Irish music
spins between games.

One day,
Irish Dad tells his Irish Boy
that today
Irish Boy can help fix the car.
Irish Boy is excited to get to help fix the car.
Irish Boy ends up
mostly holding the flashlight.
Irish Boy is underwhelmed
and has a short attention span.
He hears old Irish music reel out of the cassette
and fill the garage
like the
      smoke
                in Irish Grandma's bar.

Irish Dad says,
"Hey, keep the light here."
Irish Boy asks,
"What is war?"
Irish Boy asks,

"Why did they stop fighting to
bury their friends
and then go back to fighting?"
Irish boy asks,
"What's a turkey shell?"

Irish Dad puts down the socket wrench.

Irish Boy asks,
"What's worse than dying?"

Irish Dad says,
"Son," he says,

"war is a terrible thing.

It's a special kind of hell.

It makes boys

shoot guns at other boys

even if they don't want to."

"But why do they do it if they don't want to?"

"Sometimes they have to.

Sometimes grown ups tell them to.

Sometimes

I don't know."

I'm really sad,

"But why?"
I'm really confused,
"Why do the grown ups do that?"
I'm really scared,
"Dad, what's worse than dying?"

Dad says,
"Love is the most important.

When it's taken away

a big part of you is taken away.

A part you need.

And sometimes just sadness fills up

what was there."

I'm quiet.

Dad is quiet.

Irish Boy
holds the flashlight back up
shines where Irish Dad needs it.

Irish Dad smiles
tired.

Irish Dad fixes the car.

Cue
"The Band Played Waltzing Matilda"
Liam Clancy

... and the young people ask me
what are they marching for
and I ask myself the same question.

EVEN IF THEY DON'T WANT TO

The current standard issue US military assault rifle is the M4 Carbine. It fires a projectile roughly the size of a number two pencil head at approximately three times the speed of sound. Due to its extremely high velocity, upon entering the human body, it creates a shockwave causing something called 'cavitation' utterly obliterating all bone and soft tissue in a space ten times the size of the bullet.

It breaks every bone on its way out
the broken backbone backdoor it punched for itself.

Doesn't even wipe its feet.

Takes whatever it wants.

Sloppy fucking thief.

At what hollow point
did this become human
achievement?

KIRBY ELEMENTARY

The cops showed up and found maybe twenty or thirty of us behind the school that night.

"You don't belong here. This is trespassing. Leave now." They sounded stern, annoyed. You could smell badge on their bully breath.

I'm pretty sure Marky had just finished his set. One acoustic guitar had been passed from band to band the whole night. It had felt so tangible. Guitar strings sewing a community together right in front of our voices. It felt like footing.

"Get the hell out of here."

Our seams groaned. We reluctantly stood. Some ran, their safety pin joints stretching.

"Go home or you'll be arrested."

As we walked away, trying our best not to unravel, Casey was holding his ground, staring needles right through the eyes of one of the cops.

"If they weren't here, most of these kids would be doing drugs or getting into actual trouble somewhere else, assholes. Sorry we were doing something positive with our time."

"Shut up and go home."

He shut up
eventually.

We left.

We didn't go home.

DRINKING TOWN WITH A SPORTS PROBLEM

Midwest goes, "How are ya?"
Midwest goes, "Did jeet yet?"
Midwest goes, "Have some puppy chow and a pop."
Midwest goes, "It's over by there."
Midwest goes, "Sorry."
Midwest goes, "Well that's nothing putting on your gym shoes and getting some fresh air can't fix."
Goes, "We don't talk about that."
Goes, "Therapy?"
Goes, "Did jeet yet?"

Midwest goes, "How ya been?"
Midwest goes, "I don't know about that."
Midwest goes, "That's not dinner conversation."
Midwest goes, "Sorry."
Goes, "Your gym shoes are in the front room closet."
Goes, "Did jeet yet?"
Goes, "Have a drink."
Goes, "Sorry."
Goes, "We're gonna go watch the game."
Goes, "Wanna come with?"
Goes, "Sorry."
Goes, "Take care."

Midwest goes, "What's all this therapy talk?"
Midwest goes, "Did jeet yet?"
Midwest goes, "I don't know, put it in the junk drawer."
Midwest goes, "Sorry."
Midwest goes, "Keep that to yourself now."
Midwest goes, "Can ya run out tuh Jewels?"
Goes, "It's not polite to talk about that."
Goes, "Sorry."
Goes, "The game is on."
Goes, "Have a drink."

Goes, "Sorry."
Goes, "Eat something, wouldja."
Goes, "Sorry."
Goes, "Have a drink."
 "Have a drink."
 "Sorry."
 "Sorry."
 "Sorry."
 "Sorry."
 "Sorry."
 "Drink."
 "Drink."
 "Sorry."

DORM ROOM, WINTER '05

he wouldn't let me leave

his hands pressed   bruises in my arms
he dropped
        to his knees

and with that he pul
              led down my pants
and with that he
              pulled down my trust
and with that he
              pulled down authority
he pulled
        down the walls
        and the flag poles
pulled down
        the plans
pulled
   down the years
pulled down the
        tuning

                        dropped it

pulled
   straight and narrow off its tracks
pulled
   pickets from the fences
   whites from eyes
pulled
   "what's the point of this shit"
   from the post holes
pulled
   my eyelids up at night
pulled

    my eyelids down in intimacy
pulled
    doors op en
    please leave the door open
pulled
    the curtains on the sun
pulled
    open cans
pulled
    open bottles
pulled
    from bottles
pulled
    from bottles
pulled
    from bottles
pul
    led
        do
                wn my jaw
pulled
    and plucked my throat
    plucked honesty can't stop pouring from these pulled down dams
pulled
    o f f the dusty sheets on the box of knives
    like abra-ka-fucking-dabra
    you can't disappear
    you can't hide in the smoke or the mirror
    stop sawing assistance in half

I pulled off the hair on the sides of my head
pulled off the sleeves on my t-shirts and jacket
pulled down "punk is dead"
pulled down "you're too old for this"
left salvation in a straightener and hairspray
in bloody fingertips on a guitar
and survival flung from my vocal power chords

left a part of me that was my choice
that was mine

that no one could pull down

left a part of me that was my choice
that was mine
that no one could pull down

left a part of me that was my choice
that was mine
that no one could pull down

JOLIET 29

This is seasonal work
I spend a good amount of my time
sweeping in the plant
cleaning up after the insulators

Kick up clouds of coal dust
Kick up clouds of calsil
Kick up a sweat for it all to stick to
on my face
under the hard hat
the heavy coat
my dad's old boots

I sweep and sweep
trying to shove it all out
Trying to get the bristles into the cracks in the concrete
where more dust hides in the foundation

In the break trailer
I try to wipe all the black dust and dirt off of me

stain towels black

blow my nose

stain towels black

The harder I work
to get all the dust out
all dark parts swept away
kept out of sight
the more they cling to the foundation
the more they find their way deeper inside me
until they can't be kept in
until I choke
and cough it all up on the floor

WHEN ASKED WHY I LISTEN TO MUSIC WHERE "THEY SCREAM SO MUCH"

There are days
when I choke on my own voice
and my words are unreadable through tears
or night sweats
or memories
or silence
and I need someone else to scream them
for me

the louder
the better.

Cue
"Bad Mouth"
Fugazi

You can't be what you were
so you better start being
just what you are...

JUNIOR MINTS

It seemed like Grandma Burke always had Junior Mints on her.
Anytime, anywhere
at the bar
at home
wherever
she had some for us kids.
A little bit of sweetness in her pocket
to share with the world.

When I was sixteen or seventeen I was a pallbearer at her funeral.
My cousins and I white glove strained to carry
her
a coffin
a pack of Virginia Slims in her pocket
a rosary wrapped around her wrist
a can of Old Style in one hand
and a box of Junior Mints in the other.

This still sits with me
sleeps with me sometimes.
My own pockets suddenly pedestals
monuments
altars to hold what will define me in death.

My eyes close
and I am lying in pine.

A single Camel Light in my pocket
flipped upside down to make it lucky like I learned.
A rosary wraps around my wrist
even though I've never been a very good Catholic
giving up lent for lent
but always trying to make my parents happy.

I spill whiskey on one hand
and hold a box of Junior Mints in the other.

Every time
I'm wearing an Easter Sunday suit
woven from every one of my broken guitar strings
soaked forever
in beer
and bruises
and basements
in blood
and rage
and passion
in community
and love
and dead heroes.

My coffin is cushioned with every first kiss
from the 8th grade timid dance
to the parking lots
to the couches
to the one in the alley on the North Side in the rain
where I dropped my jacket and went for it.

My body rests in every time my heart pounded
hard enough to make sparks
start fires
burn down porches
and bridges
in one skipped beat.

The air in the coffin is shoved out
replaced with newspaper rolls
ready to be thrown
and make my wish come true to
break windows with words.
Spray paint cans begin to pile.
KEVIN WAS HERE is stenciled on my eyelids.

Regrets find their way in
   things get crowded things get stuffy things get in the way
   I am slowly buried beneath them
   held under by the weight of so many things

and I don't want it
any of it.

I hope for space.
I hope for enough room for something to grow
out of what's left

like flowers growing out of horse shit.

When my eyes open again
I shake it off best I can
and grab hold of all that's left.
I smile in stories about Old Style
and Junior Mints to share.

I think back to sixteen or seventeen.

I think back to a lost boy
trying so hard to find a way
to be a good man
a good person
good

and hoping it's not too hard to
carry.

GRADUATION

and the caps hit the floor
and the gowns are hung up to collect dust
and the economy is hemorrhaging
and work at the scaffold yard and power plants is drying up
and a kid from school who went to war is still dead

and you move to Austin, TX
and it's with your college friends
and it's because there's jobs there
and there's still silver screen dreams there
and they're all for the picking and chasing
and you eventually learn

and your move ends a decent relationship
and you date more
and it's exercises in undeveloped judgement
and bad timing you never explain
and it's a mess like you
and you eventually learn

and so you keep writing
and it keeps you afloat
and the band is gone
and you're alone on a stage
and your Screeching Weasel shirt fades
and you eventually learn

and you keep moving
and eventually

it's forward

Cue
"What We Worked For"
Against Me!

Do we only need to keep working because it pays rent?
Sleeping under plastic stars glued to a ceiling
Muscles burning alcohol & nicotine
every morning...

AUSTIN, TX

The first time I met Austin
it was at some backyard party
full of Christmas lights
free tacos
and beer with too much fucking hops.

I went to shake hands with Austin
but he tried way too hard
to awkwardly give ill-fitted daps
that didn't match the effort
he put into seeming effortlessly laid back.

I said aren't you too old
to be double fisting drinks
and reckless in your hands
but he just mumbled
something about endless summers and swimming holes.

Trying to be charming
he quickly changed the subject
told me he's been working on a screenplaynovelalbumshortwebseriesstart-upapp
every day for the last eight years
but hasn't started yet
then got really defensive
and told me to wait outside in traffic
while he finishes building this condo.

After this I watch him night in and night out
grip his gutters
and puke up one dollar shots and VIP wristbands
and you can bet the yellow in his eyes
he still looks sharp doing it too.

Over and over
I watch him

wink in the mirror.

Over and over
Austin tilts back bottles and raises cranes.

Over and over
drunk on himself
drunk on tonight
drunk on this velvet rut
this Neverland
this blind chase down glass necks
convincing himself he is still young
and fresh
and smalltown
and in control
and I don't know whether or not to be angry
or jealous.

PLEASE PROVIDE YOUR EMPLOYMENT HISTORY

When asked about previous employment
I tell them I worked in a haberdashery.
Once I convince them it is a real word, they continue with questions.

When asked about the job itself
I tell them I worked as the hatter.
Second hand hats, brand new hats, I explain how I spent years trying on hats for myself.

When asked about the hats I wore
I tell them I wore every hat you could imagine.
Tried on so so many hats. Sweated through so so many brims.

When asked why I let myself eventually live in the haberdashery
I tell them I needed to find what fit, so I worked days and nights in different hats.
Four the life of me, I couldn't find a hat that fit, lasted, that didn't make me feel like I sold out.

When asked if I enjoyed all the hats
I tell them I didn't enjoy the taste of mercury.
Pent up in there like the king of hats with no crown to show for it.

Wore my fingers to poison.

Made it hard to hold anything.

Made the feeling at the tips leave.

Made the feeling at the joints leave.

Made me leave.

Made me leave.

Made me leave.

Made me leave.

DAY TWO

I come from a long line of bartenders
sweat-breakers
broken backs from digging ditches
and a few teachers.

Mom taught math
Sis' teaches english
and Dad
told us stories.

All of this spins around in my mind
and I can see it spinning faster and faster
in the eyes of the student
whose face is only inches from mine
as he says,
"What are you gonna do about it if I don't,"
all pufferfish
pointy-chested
as the rest of the high school class waits.

Waits
as I feel the ink
beneath my long sleeves
buttons
and slacks
begin to burn.

Waits
as my first moshpit-branded brain begins to boil.

Waits as I keep back the gasoline bile
and get all choked up on
the hand grenade pins and needles
that have been planted in my throat
and grown a drum set in my jawbone
I play

in time
with swaying picket signs.

But today

I muted it.

I'm proud of this kid.

I want to tell him this.
I want to tell him I'm glad
that after thirteen years of learning,
the one thing he has not picked up on
is to blindly follow authority.
I want to tell him this.
I want to tell him I'm sorry.
I'm sorry you're stuck in a broken system
where men in designer suits
who have never seen a classroom
keep cutting art out of the heart
of education
because you can't express yourself
properly or profitably enough
through the color by letters
number two pencil
piss poor pointillistic painting
like A, B, C, or D all of the above
is being held above all else.
I want to tell him all of this.
I want to say I'm sorry,
but it all comes out as

"Sit down."

Sit down.

Save your strength.
Hold on to that crumpled paper, homemade bomb heart
that keeps blasting shards of
chicken scratch shrapnel

through your bloodstream.

Hold on to this
like sandbags for a really rainy day.

I know it hurts.
It did and still does for me,
but there's a difference between
picking a fight
and picking your fights.

Sit down.
This one's not worth it.
I'm temporary, kid.
I'm gone from your life by the end of this period.
Then I'm off to who knows where
to substitute
all of their authority
and none of the mutual respect.
All of their authority
and none of the time.
All of their authority
and none of the real chances
to make you listen,
so listen now:

Sit down.
A cop's not going to be so polite, kid.
You'll get nothing less than a slap on the jaw
with a nightstick.
Sit down.
There's something to be said for political captives,
but there's not much valor in a detention slip.
Sit down

and stand up for something worth it.
Stand strong for something worth it
but for now
sit down.

I'm sorry.
I'm tired.
I spent all of yesterday
in a gang graffiti soaked, in-school suspension classroom
squared off with a seventh grade girl
with more balls than either of us would know what to do with,
and a blade in her backpack for the walk home.

This tough guy act doesn't scare me.
Forchristsake, you're wearing 3D glasses with the lenses popped out—
how am I supposed to take you seriously right now?
But seriously, you might not get it now
and you probably think
I'm just another asshole with a name tag
telling you what to do,
but I swear
from the bottom of the bricks and spray paint in my belly,
that when I'm saying
"sit down",
I am praying

you learn what it means
to stand up.

A SINCERE TOAST

So, money, right?
So long as people are making it we're good, right?
So long as the people in charge are making it, we all win, right?
Because it trickles down, right?
Like a pyramid of champagne glasses, right?
It must be,
it must be like that because you drink champagne when you celebrate, right?!
And we're all gonna get rich so let's celebrate, right!?
I mean, it's not like there's any incentive for the glass at the top to make itself
   bigger, right?
Like one gigantic champagne glass?
Like a kiddie pool on a stem, right?
Like it keeps getting bigger and bigger and no champagne comes down to
   the smaller
champagne glasses that make up the vast majority of the pyramid, right?
No.
That would be ridiculous.
Why would the big champagne glass do that?
Then the rest of us couldn't celebrate all the money we're gonna make, right?
'Cause we've been told we're gonna get that champagne.
Never mind that the weight of a gigantic champagne glass full of champagne
   at the top
would put so much pressure on the other champagne glasses that we couldn't
   even
move out of the pyramid if we wanted to, right?
'Cause we're gonna get some of that champagne, right?!
It's not like that big glass on top can get any bigger, right?!
Because even if it does, we'll just get more champagne, right?
Because this whole set up
this whole pyramid
is the only way we're all gonna get some champagne, right?
That's what the folks with the big glass at the top say
and they gotta know
look at that glass!
It's so big!
So let's open more champagne!

Here!
This one's huge!
Vintage oil champagne!
There's so much fucking champagne!
Who cares if we get too drunk and drill too many holes
in our liver, right!?
Forget those smaller bottles!
There's no way the sun or wind could ever make
this much fracking
I mean fucking
champagne!
Why even bother, right!?
Or how about this one?!
Pop the precision guided cork off
that bottle of military champagne!
Look at all the champagne!
Blood might be thicker than water
but you can drink away the stains
with champagne!!!
We should buy more of these
bottles, right!?
Look at how much champagne is
in that big glass
at the top now!
There's so much
we're all getting
some now, right?!
Those glasses on the bottom
that are still empty
they're just not trying
hard enough, right?!
They're just lazy
or made of glass
or plastic
or something with
less integrity.
Whatever it is
it's different and scary.
Not like the crystal glass
at the top!

Why can't they just be like
the glass at the top?!
That's what we're
all trying to do, right?!
We've just gotta
make ourselves
out of crystal!
Right!
Any other way
of doing things
would be a
terrifying idea!
That big glass
at the top is
afraid of any
other idea
and they have
such a big glass
of so much
champagne
that they
must be right
right?!
So there's
nothing wrong with
being scared
and killing
or locking up
anyone
who disagrees
right!?
Right!
And we should
celebrate
getting rid
of those
scary scary
different
small
glasses!

Unscrew
this bottle of
prison
industrial
champagne!
There
it is!
The more
we're afraid
and the more
we put
behind
bars
and the
more
we build
to kill
and spill
the more
champagne
there
is
right?!
Right!
So
cel
ebrate!
Dri
nk
up!
We'
re
go
nna
be
rich!
We'
re
go
nna

be
rich!

Every

one

of

us

rich

Cue
"The Deadly Rhythm"
Refused

We consume our lives like we are thankful
for what we are being forced into...

THE SHAME BANK

You didn't grow up with much money
had more in common with the Winslows or Bundys
than the Taylors on Home Improvement
but your dad went to night classes in his forties
while you and Lisa were in high school
and eventually got those promotions
so when it was time to leave the nest
there was a small safety net.
In case of emergency
there was some money to catch you.

The fridge would empty
bills would stack
meals would be skipped
and eventually a phone call could be made
to the shame bank

You assumed when you hit adulthood
You'd know it
You'd wear it proud
You'd have adult thoughts
You'd have things "figured out"

but the only thing you've figured out
is that all along
all the grown ups
were making it up as they went
as much as us kids

they're playing make-believe
in more convincing costumes.

You write about it
make ink slippery grip on control
while the mail piles
while bank statements read

is this it?
is this all you'll do?
are you doomed to stumbling up
and falling down stairwells?

sleeping in debt?

accruing guilt and interest?

pretending it's all okay?

pretending it won't happen again?

pretending you have a back up plan?

I SAID FUCK OFF I'LL TALK LATER

It's heavy
this air
waking up
moving
chewing on vocal chords and anger
all fucking day.
Keeping a lid on a pressure cooker
all the damn time.

I know the density of drywall way too well.
I know who wins in screaming contests with walls.

I'm tired
of myself
of this dumb body
clumsy fists
sore eyes
and I want my pillow
to not just keep my mouth from waking the neighbors.

Cue
"Nausea"
Jeff Rosenstock

I got so tired of discussing my future
I started avoiding the people I love...

THESAURUS

Our feet felt like they skipped inside our laughs,
like stones skipping on the streetlight,
spilt across the asphalt.

We caught ourselves on my car.

"You're amazing," skipped out of my dumb smile
and before our lips could meet
you said, "You need to get yourself a thesaurus."

So I fuckin' did.

You are

amazing
awesome
marvelous
incomprehensible
wonderfully kickass
astoundingly unbelievable
earth-shaking, knee-quaking
pants-crappingly fantastic
intergalactically remarkable
firework glow on our cheeks lit with the sparks
we kick out of the dirt that gems like us have been living in
you are you
you are you
the most incredible thing about you is you

and you smile back

and I dare you to let me keep going

but you kiss me instead.

UNHINGED

Nitroglycerin is used as a vasodilator to treat heart attacks and the chest pain that accompanies the loss of oxygen to the myocardial tissue. In other words, it opens the blood vessels of the heart to allow for better circulation. It is also one of the main ingredients in dynamite.

You wish you were drunk
or still with her
or still had everything that was stolen through a broken window
or still had the job you sacrificed for
or still with her
or drunk

or something more
than numb
teeth and knuckles spraying all over the apartment walls.

Tried to do what you've always done.
Tried to do what home taught you.
Tried to do what you watched your dad do.
Tried to keep it inside and out of sight.

Tried to keep it under your tongue
hoping to ease your chest
but ended up losing your security deposit
ended up blasting a quarry in your throat
ended up flooding it with novocaine

ended up only able to give half a smile
with what's left.

DROP (excerpt)

I would kiss an anchor into you
if it meant you would stay.

HUNTING FOR LOST TREASURE (WE WON'T FIND)

The feeling is always there
in a dimly lit back corner at least
but it sometimes takes losing something
for it to grab you by the back of the neck.

They smashed the driver's side window with a big rock.
It was still lying on the street peppered with tempered glass.
It was Thanksgiving morning.
My car had been gutted and cleaned out.

The police suggested checking garbage cans nearby.
While I'd likely never see the laptop again
there's no reason for them to keep all the poetry notebooks.
No value in them, the cop said.

To her credit, Vanessa did her best to keep my spirits up.
Took her roommate's dog with to help us look.
The dog smiled the way dogs do and licked my hands.
It helped a little.

You don't really think about
how many trash cans are in your neighborhood until you're looking in every one
wishing you'll see the last five years looking back at you,
but only seeing more garbage.

The world seems so small and familiar
until you're looking for something lost.
Until you know it's out there somewhere you will never find.
Until the sun sets and burns a hole in the horizon.

As the world begins to expand around you
racing for the edges of your sight
you begin to collapse into something smaller

and smaller and smaller still

the town
the block
the street
the garbage

the job I lost
the new apartment to save money
the packed car now empty

the boy looking for a woman who was already gone though he won't admit it

the dog pulling an arm on its leash

all ready to be swallowed up somewhere.

DRIVE

i want to die

i want to die

i want   to die

i want to   die
that tree could   do it
i want to   die
that light pole looks strong enough
i   want to die
i want   to die

i want to

i want to

i drive
s e v e   n   t   y   in a residential
with a silent brok   en radio
i hear the pistons   punching   proclaiming
i want
       to die
not a car
don't ruin someone else's car
don't ruin   someone else's   life
i don't want to hurt   anyone else
don't do this   to anyone else
i want   to die
       alone
i'll die alone

    i want to die
    i want to die

with the pedal

        to the floor
with windshield

with

                                        ejection

with tempered glass necklace
with airbag pyrotechnics
without a seatbelt

                  loud
                  hard
                  and mine

                  mine

                  my choice

                  i want this

from the back of my throat
to the split veins in my temple

                  i want this

i want this crash for the silence

        i want to die
        i want to die

there's nothing left   to lose
i haven't lost already

        i want to die

        she's better off   without me

they're better off without me
they're all better off without me
without my flaws on full blast
in their mouths

                                                                                                      i'll just go

                                                                             i'll go
                                                                      i'll drive
                                                          i'll die
                      i'll die and they'll be relieved

                I'll die and they won't have to deal with me anymore

                                    they don't want to deal with me anymore

that's why no one listened
that's why no one noticed

drive
  f   a   s   t   e   r
                          die
                                    f   a   s   t   e   r

           drive faster die faster

                                        faster

                                                                  faster

        d i e

                d i e

                        d i e

Then the phone rings.
I pull over and weep when the phone rings.
I hear, "I'm worried about you."

                                      It sounds like sure footing.

I want to drive.
I drive home.

I CONVINCE MYSELF I DON'T BELIEVE IN GHOSTS SO I CAN GET SOME SLEEP

Finality.
I've seen it.
It happens

but I still wonder about things like afterlife
heaven
hell
still believe in ghosts
and will swear to this day that me and Mike saw what we saw that night
between the trees
outside the car window
as we drove down Archer Ave

but things come to an end
even if you believe in another chapter

chapters still end
and

what we had is gone

took me too long to let go

to
forgive the rain
forgive the dark
forgive the trees

to
forget chapters
forget myself
let this ghost be a trick of the eyes

and keep driving.

THE LAST POEM I'LL WRITE ABOUT THE MESS WE MADE

It turned unhealthy
and I caked too much stage makeup on it
I ordered the stage hands rope burn to keep the curtain from falling
I kept the applause going too long
I let palms sting.

I'm sorry.
Thank you.
Take a bow.

Selfishness went home
and forgiveness finally filled the seats.

I've held onto what's left of the good.
I've let all the bad go
save for the lessons learned
changes that needed to be made.

I can listen to *We Shall All Be Healed* again
and smile
and let the record spin.

I'll see you when I see you.
If I don't, I hope you're well.

Cue
"Slow West Vultures"
The Mountain Goats

(Let the record play until the hissing
starts to skip.)

ON SMASHING A GUITAR
(CAN BE PLAYED WITH D, A, AND G)

This is not a spectacle for the stage.
It belongs in the middle of every hull in the room.
It should be as a viking funeral.

Splintered neck and shattered head will gain-cranked
wood-ripple the cracked concrete waters
as cigarette cherry arrows shot from broken strings
turn you into a pyre
basement fire
smoke so thick
you can slam-dance-stutter-stumble
up it
struggling the whole way to keep your footing
on the ground soaked in
beer
sweat
and twenty-something teen angst.

Even the straight edge kids will crack a smile.

This is blood blister beautiful.
This is sinking ship release.
This is ramshackle freedom.

You are nothing to apologize for.

Don't clean up the mess.

FOR SHANE
FOR THE IRISH THAT
KEEPS HIM STANDING
AND THE IRISH IN ME

Your teeth didn't rot from your head.
It wasn't erosion or decay
they just got in the way.
Your words had to kick them out
like pub windows.
Your gums just slowed you down like mud on boots.

Shane,
your mouth is a whiskey barrel of a gun
loaded
your voice a slurred solace
giving this rot such sweet smells.

In the 1970's and 80's
the violence of what the Irish (in true form)
refer to as The Troubles peaked.
Our time will come concussed cobbled streets
and choirs of hunger struck prison walls to death.
In a time when to be called Irish
was bloody
spit-soaked
and hated
a group of kids
fueled by the Celtic urge to self-destruct
had the audacity to sing.

Shane,
you had the audacity
to swallow up all that hurt into your mouth
to grind reels
to chomp hornpipes

and chew up jigs

then puke it all back out like red roses
sucker punch enamel to the pulp
crack crowns
and spit the pieces at the throne
smile gaping and howling all the while.

You played loud
played fast
and rocked the walls of London pubs
with something other than bombs.
You spewed Irish thump guts dance music
joyful defiance that bypassed intellect
tossed brains to the curb
and hit hearts in the throat.

The whole band
fell around the world
spilled swaggering beauty
from such a shambling wreck.
You showed the continents your contents
throwing up bottles and biting blood into the crowd

but they didn't understand it, Shane.
The rest of the world didn't get it.
My neighborhood still doesn't.

They know green beer and fucking Bennigan's.
They know shamrocks and marshmallow rainbows.
They're still taken with the Clancy Brother's clean white sweaters
and clean white music

not
broken glass and Belfast
not the pieces scattered at the peace walls.

How can they know
that when you sang
you prayed

to the old gods of gut-rot and wells
of bile and busted lips
your hands throbbing
gripping a microphone like a rosary that's gone cold

your mouth open
for every swig
of sadness
trying to fill the holes in history
that still stain spirits?

You screamed amen
blowing your
teeth into the air like bricks
while your throat rattled like riot shields.

I know
it's not the whiskey that has left you
blue-skinned and wet-brained
clutching a mic stand to stay
standing.

It's the scarred and cratered road you took
chasing ghosts down the gutter
fumbling to make them stay one more day
that broke your heart
and made your mouth turn to mush.

WHAT WE WORK
(EXCERPT)

I would like to draw your attention to the fact that children
are among an extremely small group of people
who can pull something like
standing up in a shopping cart
as their parents push through aisles of produce
and yell, "I AM A ROCKET SHIP!!!"
and mean it
and not be politely asked to leave by security
more than once.

BtMI

To the nights I stood ready to open-mouth kiss porcupines
I played pincushion so well

there were couch cushions
stuffed full of cigarette cherries and headlines
waiting for us to fall asleep
and burn the whole goddamn body down

to the nights flirting with the inevitable
and fucking the moment instead
steering wheel tears
tempered glass tantrum
and the open arms of light poles

to the nights I wanted to die

You don't own me.
You don't own me.

In 2005 the ska-punk band
The Arrogant Sons of Bitches
disassembled when the members of the band
followed the need to "get real jobs."
All of them but frontman Jeff.
Jeff Rosenstock instead
continued to make music
and instead
ended up living in his parent's basement

it was cold it was damp it was dark
but we are nothing if not reactions against our own environment

You don't own me. You don't own me.

Jeff, I'm baseball bat to bar stool
and brick wall boxing again

my hands are bleeding again
beating again
I'm left shuffling through splinters
and not eating again

Jeff, it's hard to see how you handled it
how you handled all the heartscrape
the hops
the hotbox
and I can't stop this
shuttering and bonebruising.

I just want to sleep, Jeff.
I just want to stop yelling, "Stop crying asshole" into mirrors, Jeff.
I just want to dream
that my blood hasn't dreamt of running to the waters
and leaving me
like this
swirling
and
drained.

The thing no one ever tells you about depression
is it has nothing to do with being sad.

It's feeling hollow
thin
empty eggshell
with rice paper walls

I don't know how to slow down most nights but I know I could get so much reading done if I got laid-up in the ICU

You don't own me.
You don't own me.

Jeff
you overloaded the outlets

you frayed your chords
let sparks fly to light up this basement
you used your busted ass laptop as kindling

because you needed this, Jeff
but now I need this
we all need this sometimes.

So let us swing guitar and duct tape into the dampness.
We will punch our shadows in their dark parts.
We'll take every shitty high school metaphor
about razor blades and wrists
stuff them into an amplifier
and let 'em rattle
then use it to carve the grooves
into this here vinyl
seven-inch

there— all the heartscrape
all the problems
climbing every towering inferno deep-burn in love
every self-inflicted car wreck
the well intentioned pileup
the break
up
the break
in
the five years of writing: gone.
job: terminated
direction spinning
skeletons scribbling

ink

to paper

ink on this paper

my problems are ink on this paper

My problems don't look so big on this eight and a half by eleven inch
piece of paper.

Here in the grooves of this vinyl
carved with a gut wrench
and a muscle still clenched the size of your fist

they sound just like this

And if I wasn't a fat kid in high school
I would have never listened to punk rock.

And if I knew how to throw a football
I would have never played any music.

And if I never got my heart broken
I would sing blah blah fucking nothing.

I would sing nothing
and I'm grateful to sing.

I'm grateful that every single day
every single one of us
every single time that we breathe
we sing an anthem of survival

the soundtrack of going down singing.

Thank you for this.

Thank you for the sure footing.

Thank you.

THE MOMENT YOU'RE AT A PUNK SHOW (OR ANYWHERE REALLY) AND DON'T KNOW THE WORDS

and realize only the singer barely does
and realize the rest are trying their best like you
and realize you're not alone in this panicked need
    to be part of something
and realize later that this is how most of life goes
and realize wearing composure is the saddest, funniest joke
    and we're all singing too loud to hear the punchline.

EIGHT STRING LULLABY

Some times,
more than anything,
I wish I could be like strings.

Tuned.
Tightened.
Taught.

Eight of them, like a mandolin,
hanging in the wind chimes
so I could slip
my song through the chip
in their window
when they need to hear it most.

His closed front gate
was a gateway drug.
Now his drug of choice
is locked doors.
Most mornings,
he wakes up and squeezes a tube a Neosporin into each ear
just so he can hear
what healing sounds like.
He says it drowns out the judgment,
says it takes the edge off the hit
of the word "faggot".

Last night he said it felt like the stars were only falling
to smash our windshields in.

Meanwhile
        across town

                                        she
falls into bed,
feeling like a drumhead

all stretched out and beaten on—
amazed she didn't break this time,
after being speed bag   bounced
simply because she was there
and dry
and worried
and said something
when she saw all those empty bottles
and bloodshot
wakeup on the front room couch.

Their lips will taste of knucklespit.

This is it.

This is when I wish.

Wish I could sing like strings,
and be there
for him or her
or anyone else
who's ever felt the back of a belt for being different—

all the other kids out there with way more guts than me
who live with their closet doors kicked
     down
letting corkscrew skeletons proudly parade out—

or all the other ones,
who only know the four walls of home
in pictures
of furniture arrangements in Ikea junk mail catalogues.

I want to eightstring sing to them.
I want to hold their body to mine,
kiss the Brillo out of their throat,
swallow all their salt,
and show them
they can still harmonize.
Show them

there is no such thing as hopeless.

There's a feeling called loneliness,
but there is never such a thing as being alone.

Do not write yourself off,
and not on a mirror.
I don't care how pretty your lipstick penmanship is,
suicide cursive still looks ugly on your reflection.

And if you've written that note,
I dare you to redraft it.

Redraft it until it reads spite.
Redraft it until it reads smiling.
Redraft it until it reads living
and living
and living
and living well is the best revenge
on those hard times
that we loyally blistergrip.

In the name of the sharpened Broken Spokes
and 3A.M. hammereds that chiseled me
safety-pin-stitch welded me,

to all the love
the rage
the stubbornness

the hip hop that swath-swagger-splinted me
to the same punk-drunk
love-punched
jukebox tunes
over and over and over again
that remind me to rock—
I will spit sparks to shock,
take stock,
with my pen loaded and my paper cocked,

and give you

everything I've got.

I will bleed   you everything I've got.

It ain't much.

It's just a couple of words,

some old wounds

I will open them.
I will press my secrets to yours.
I will bleed you this.
Pour you poetry.
It's donated blood.

I hope it helps you   heal.

I hope it helps her laugh, even a little
and leave.

I hope it helps him   sleep,
bedroom unlocked,   door open

so I can sing to him
these eight stringed lullabies.
More than anything—

I wish

this:

AGAIN. LOUDER. LET THE NEIGHBORS COMPLAIN.

I woke up this morning
yesterday is dead and I am still standing
I am still breathing
I am still alive
I'm alive

therefore

I am better than yesterday

and yes
I don't always know what I'm doing
and it's a little rough around the edges
there's blood stains on my jeans
and mud caked on my boots
burns scarred on my hands
and what else is new
I'm still alive and

I am better than yesterday

and I'm still learning
I'm still practicing
drinking lighthouse on the rocks
and smiling safe passage
into the mirror
every morning
and it's silly
but it sure as hell tastes better
than eating six feet of dirt
on purpose
and I'm still alive and

I'm better than yesterday

and my blood
still shares the same salinity as the ocean
and I'm learning to take cues from the size of what's inside of me
and push and flow
bruise and slick
break and crash
and know that no matter what
I am capable of being whole again
if I just give it time
and let the tide come back in
and I'm still alive and

better than yesterday

and everyday
over and over
make this mess into mosaic
and don't clean it up
but plaster it in place
and make it dance floor
and make it shining armor
and make it spectacle in the sunlight

and make it better than yesterday

and I woke up this morning
and yesterday is dead and I am still standing
I am still breathing
I am still alive
I'm alive

I am better than yesterday
I am better than yesterday
I am better than yesterday

Cue
"Syke! Life is Awesome!"
Bomb the Music Industry

(Scream the whole damn song.
Repeat until your throat hurts & your
chest doesn't.)

GREEN GILLS LEARN TO BREATHE

"The great Gaels of Ireland are the men that God made mad,
For all their wars are merry, and all their songs are sad."
                                            -G.K. Chesterton

The first time I smoked a cigar was at Grandma Burke's wake.
My uncle built a bar in his basement and
the family built the smoke in the air and
the drinks on the lips and
the laughter on the ceiling.

The first time I burned my throat was in my uncle's basement.
My aunts laughed saying, "You look green," and
the family patted my green back and
the drinks green were emptied and poured green again and
the green laughter followed me to the bathroom green.

The first time I inhaled the world honest was green in a smoke-filled room green.
My father was whiskey-smiling green with a cigarette in green hand and
the family made green mirth out of green throat lumps green and
the drinks green became a green conduit green and
the laughter green carried green us forward green

mourning this way
living this way
knowing that in the end
the world will break our green hearts and
we will pick up the green pieces and
smile green smiles

SIXTEEN PINTS LATER

Ladies and gentlemen and those not adhering to the gender binary in this
    fine establishment,
before you get shit faced tonight
and wake up tomorrow
with the morning dried up on your eyelids
a belly full of steel wool
mouth stuffed with nine volt batteries
and porcelain under your fingernails that kept the room from spinning

take a breath

take a break

from drinking

entirely   for a year   trust me

and sing all of the following sober.

Play DD every time your friends go out.
They will love you for it.
You may hate them a little for the night
but they will love you for as long as there is shout in their lungs.

Go to parties.
Ridiculous parties.
Lava spewing, vesuvial ragers
where everyone is fucked up
and looking to fuck or get fucked up and fuck or fuck the fucked up

and Harvard grads are doing lines of blow off the kitchen counter like,
"How 'bout them apples?!"
See the best and worst of people in one night   and remember it.

Talk to a stranger at a bar.
Talk to someone knuckle in the lung beautiful.
Get their number.

Spend time with your friends
and tell your friends how much you love them
over and over and over like,
"Nah, man. I love YOU!!!"
without slurring over your own feet or stumbling your words.

Do cartwheels past the police
like they weren't terrifying.

Throw empty beer bottles
at brick walls
at dumpsters
at anything really
at cop cars
then run from the police laughing
like fear didn't have a spot in the dictionary.

Sleep on a rooftop in midwest autumn with people you love
over and over and over.

Go to shows.
Dive into the mosh pits.

Go to clubs
and dance
and dance
and dance

and give zero fucks what anybody thinks.
Do it confidently.
Then do it again and again and again
until you are drenched in glory in the middle of a dance circle
and dance like a Muppet.
Accidentally invent a dance move called The Muppet.

Then eat a 3am burrito sleep on a pool table walk them home
and finally just kiss the one you've fallen in love with
but could never muster the spine to tell them how you've felt.

Smile and recall and recant
instead of piecing it together with the sweaty pictures from the night
before.
Realize that photographs are useless
if the moments were not lived and memories not remembered

that these blackout freeze frames
might as well be rough sketches
of strangers that look just like you.

Piss yourself   and own it.

Shout in public places.

Go to a karaoke bar and fucking mean it.

Build a goddamn pillow fort.

Try something new knowing it is a completely stupid idea.

Be uncomfortable.

Be awkward.

Feel.

Live.

Laugh.

Throw up from laughing,

and laugh.

Savor every day
every weekend
and every time you want to destroy yourself,
build and create instead.

Find yourself in the sweetest of exhales.

And then

if you still want to,
but don't need to,

pull up a stool
and have a drink,

knowing there is unbridled outside of a bottle,

knowing you are capable of more than anything that can fit in a pint glass,

knowing you put the courage into this liquid,

knowing you.

Sláinte.

Cue
"IF I Should Fall From Grace with God"
The Pogues

Let me go down in the mud
where the rivers all run dry...

I WILL SCREAM THIS 'TIL WE'RE ALL DEAD

To all the people you've heard say that a good relationship is the worst thing that can happen to a poet and their work,

sorry, but shut the fuck up.

Frankly you need to get out more or at least read a fucking book like *Leaves of Grass* or some inspiring shit like that.

Let a crisp autumn breeze take you.
The warm lips of someone on the tip of your chilled nose
thaw and crack the frozen lake in your guts.
Skip rocks in you.
Be shocked that you can see your breath in the cold
because you could've sworn they just took that breath away.

Hold on
to these moments.
Hold on to them like someone under the sheets
when the heater breaks
and the only thing lighting up the room
are the sparks off the L tracks just outside the window
but goddamn: you're happy to be alive

I'm happy to be alive

and warm
and have these memories
these moments
this melody to hold onto.

Now, I'm not saying you need a relationship to be happy.
That's why mosh pits, mixtapes, and fuckin' Netflix were invented.
I'm just saying

the crooked tooth in her smile deserves an entire book of lovedumb poems
like this poem.
Her stubborn South Austin accent
moves symphonies to drawl.

Me and Amanda make each other neon bar sign
glow crackle buzz
we give each other sunrise every morning
plant stars in each other's cheeks at night
open soft palms with sturdy callouses for
holding.

We work hard
for each other.
We make it worth it
for each other.

We laugh at each other's farts, and if that's not love, then fuck everything forever.

We make me
want to stand on a table in a fancy restaurant full of cardboard people on beige
boring-ass dates, and go, "Y'all are fuckin' up! Y'all just exchange
pleasantries and digest, then have routine, expected sex and repeat!"
I just boosted her over a no trespassing fence.
She just finished the stencil while I shook the spray cans.
I put the pedal to the floor
while her middle finger is to the law
and the cash is flying out the back windows
in the cloud of dust we kicked up behind us
and yes

this is hyperbole!

And yes, we go to fancy restaurants too.

Set to a lung-top-sing-along soundtrack
of guilty pleasure pop-punk-trash
in the middle of a Walgreens toothpaste aisle
and side-eye from the staff

she gives me life.
She gives me worlds.
She gives me poetry.

Every sly grin a stanza.
Every wink a line.
Every flutter a word.

She's got lightning bugs in her laughter, y'all
and bluebonnets in the soles of her feet.

When it feels like there's nothing left to trust
there is still this stillness
the air
between our lips
the ground
beneath our feet
and the things she grows from it all.

She grows food and foundation, y'all.
I'd swear she's got that good dirt and rainwater in her blood
and keeps firm grip on life in her breath.

Despite the memories and stories told in scars
every blood-soaked page I've written or read
the holes drilled in with the drywall dust
all innards brought out

she reminds me there's more worth writing.

The page can make bloody into bloodier

but it can make bloodier into beautiful
beautiful into speechless
she makes beautiful into speechless

into lightning bugs

into seeds on the wind.

Makes it look easy.

WE SLEEP WELL TOGETHER

She speaks night light
and reminds me how to dream in the dark.

WHAT KEEPS US TOGETHER

I heard somewhere that gravity affects time. The further from Earth's pull, the faster time moves. The closer to the gravitational pull, the slower time moves.

"I can't wait to build a life with you."
"Okay."

We gathered up our things and walked to the tallest mountain. Our fingers interlocked and our palms folded into paper airplanes that drifted us to the top of the highest peak of the highest mountain. Along the way up, our feet kissed the crowns of trees and made them bloom into bells, bloom a roof, bloom all nine yards of rain and light until our toes touched the top of the mountain and we lived our life together as fast as avalanche. Fast as the rushing wind at the peak. But it was cold there. Cold with all that wind and time rushing away. There was no time to wait, no time to warm.

"I want to hold a moment with you as long as we can."
"Okay."

We gathered up our things and held each other tight. Our paper airplanes unfolded and our arms fashioned a sled. We slicked down the other side of the mountain together. We came to rest in soft black dirt. A garden. Our held hands, pressed together as if to pray, folded into a shovel spade. Together we dug. As the heat grew, we gave each other the cold breeze we remembered from the mountain top. Together we dug until our shovel struck the core and rang it like a bell. We found the door inside. We carried one another across the threshold. Inside, the ringing stopped, the heat became warmth, and it was still. Time slowed to a whispered hum. Our shovel unfolded into hands. Our bodies folded into each other's bodies. Finally still. Warm. Able to hold this.

"I want to hold you like this."
"Okay."

WHAT ARE YOUR INTENTIONS

My knee lifted
from the dirt. We walked
backwards away from the water, back through the Green Belt. Our dogs jumped
into the back of the car, hind legs first. We drove
in reverse the whole way home. Home became a house as we packed
up our things and put them back in the truck. Made stops at our houses
 and unloaded.
We counted
up to midnight and celebrated
the old December once or twice. All the while, we pulled
meals from our mouths and plated
them nicely before throwing
them on the stove until they were cold and raw. Swam
backwards around Deep Eddy. I watched
the brown in your skin shine
back up to the sun. You smiled
watching Irish songs and histories fall
back into my mouth as I spit
drinks into pint after pint. We drove
in reverse to nowhere. Spent three days watching
Texas rush past us in the rear view. Watched
movies from end to beginning.

"I'm coming out of a serious relationship. Still working through it. I just
wanna hang out and see if this goes anywhere. No prior intentions."
You looked serious when you asked, "What are your intentions?" We kissed

then moved
further from each other on the couch. Your dogs jumped
off of me after slurping
the slobber off my cheeks. A few nights after this, I walked
you backwards from your friend's door to Bill's car. The four of us pulled
into Slick Willies, tail lights leading the way, where we watched balls roll
up from pockets until they touched
our cue tips. We threw
the car into reverse all the way to Hyde Park where we handed

the waitress our food and she took
our orders. We were all here because a few days after all this I deleted
your number from my phone as you listed
the number in reverse before Safi laughed
and told
the four of us to swap
numbers, said
where we were going to go on a double date, walked
away backwards before he decided to intervene before he saw
me with the courage enough to try and get your number. I had seen
you after this. I hope to see
you again.
You were a little drunk. You yelled
something about punk rock.
"You're delightful," blurted
back into my mouth still not believing you were talking to me.
I noticed you a few times after this, if I'm being honest.

Cue
"We are All Compost in Training"
Ramshackle Glory

(Yell the words with her as you waltz at
your wedding reception in the living room.)

If Freedom is doing what I want, well that means
I gotta know what that is
not just what it isn't...

OPEN YOUR EARS AND BREATHE

"I'm using the word studio in very loose terms," I said to Laura as we climbed the squealing stairs to where Jared was seated at the boards.

She normally gets paid to sing, but today generosity and excitement trumped cash. Our space was the upstairs of a little rundown house on Richardson Lane. It was rundown as in run-and-cut-your-leg-open-on-a-fence-in-the-getaway type rundown. The power was out downstairs, and a single rattling window unit was the only thing keeping the recording room on the top floor from lighting up like a torch. After all, it was Texas. The heat is oppressive here. 10,000 choirs of blow dryers seared the air outside while the sun slouched in his throne. A lazy monarch intent on moving only when he absolutely had to.

The three of us were sweat, spit, and flaking finish on the wood floors. I'd have sworn the pleather couch was sweating too with the way the light slumped into the soft cushions. We listened to the song and talked through ideas. I couldn't help the near rhythmic adjusting of my underwear. It was either riding up because of the perspiration on my legs, or it was curling up in my shorts the same way a leaf does when it's on fire.

Unfortunately, for the sake of sound, the A/C had to be turned off while recording.

"Fun."

We finished talking, and the last rattle of the window unit gave way to the barely audible cicadas panting outside. Laura stood and slipped her sandals off. Her copper-colored toes curled for a moment and stretched, trying to catch a breeze in the stagnant air.

The track rolled. She inhaled.

What I do know, is when her breath
poured from her throat
the sun was overthrown
the floor fell from below our feet
and the walls were pulled
    down

      like statues of dictators.
We were washed in amber and glow.
It didn't matter that pieces of the
headphone cushion would be stuck to our ears
when we cut and went home. It didn't matter
that I was sitting in a puddle. Even the cicadas
shut the fuck up.

We found relief.

We made
release

We
raised
holy

over

hellish

heat.

MY FAVORITE SONG

Jason Bayani wrote, "Maybe when we say love, we mean a safe place to fall apart."

Things make more sense and hurt less
with my head buried in the speakers or
my heart wrapped in headphones or
at 33 1/3 revolutions per minute or
with 6 strings or
just 3 chords or
with you texting, "I'm on my way home."

It's my favorite song.

I know all the words.
I know the liner notes by heart
and my fingers learned all the back scratches and right keys to touch.

When I wake up like I do sometimes
and scare the dogs
and the cat
the melody is there
your hands are there
to pick up the pieces
your arms to pull me back
together
your lips to quiet my sweat
your body to hold me still.

It's my favorite song

you sing it so well
and

I am so happy I survived
to hear it.

I'm so happy I am alive
to hear it in our home.

I am so happy I finally made it home.

FIRE ACADEMY TRANSLATIONS

"It's a good day today, Cadet Burke."
"Why's that, Lieutenant?"
"You learned something."

THIS IS WHAT THE VOLUME KNOB IS FOR
AFTER "DANCE MUSIC" BY THE MOUNTAIN GOATS

Burning behind the eyes
salt the teeth
splinters in the knuckles.

This is what the volume knob is for.

Spit rattle through the walls
dice the vocal cords
iron in the throat.

This is what the volume knob is for.

His fingers wrap around my dreams
crush the sleep to paste
sweat in the mattress.

This is what the volume knob is for.
This is what the volume knob is for.
This is what the volume knob is for.

This is what the volume knob is for.

Turn it 'til it breaks off
crank that shit
open it like a sink
let it wash out
the smoke
the vomit
the stinging

shower down
rinse out
clean up

stand up
when you need help
up
up
up
turn it
up
up
up

This is what the volume knob is for.

When you are drowning on air
sinking in silence

when the room is thick with empty

and you are choking on your own skin

these speakers are floodgates blown out blown open.

Your ears a life raft.
Your heart a flare gun.

This is what the volume knob is for.

It all feels better swimming in this noise
it all feels better swimming in this noise
you stop sinking and float in this noise
you float in this noise
you float in this noise
in this music
in this music
in this music
in this music
in this
in this
in this
in this
in this

this
this
this
this

this

this

this is what the volume knob is for.

Cue
"Slow Death Hymn"
Mischief Brew

If it's a highway
I am trying just to drive.
I am trying just to drive
Stay awake + stay alive.

ACKNOWLEDGEMENTS

First and foremost, thank you for your time reading this book. I sincerely hope it helped someone out there. At the very least, I hope you enjoyed the playlist.

I can never thank enough the poetry family I made here in Texas. Thank you Austin Poetry Slam, Austin Neo Soul, Mic Check, Write About Now, and Blah Blah for your continued support. Bill Moran, Zach Caballero, Jomar Valentin, Lacey Roop, Danny Strack, Ebony Stewart, Tova Charles, Zai, Amir Safi, Ariana Brown, Brian Francis, Christopher Michael, Glori B, Julian Copado, Andre Bradford, Mr. Dave, and too many more to name, y'all made Texas home. Thank you Hanif for the kind words and Derrick Brown for the inspiration and the sincere silliness. Thank you to Matt, Brad, Casey, and TJ for still being in touch and willing to be dragged to Teehan's whenever I'm back in town.

Thank you to Denise from Fistolo Records for being cool with the dedication in this book. Also, thank you Vanessa for the time and for the permission to use your name and tell my part of the story. Also thank you Gary Lovely and Allison Truj for your work on this book. Y'all are fucking gems.

Thank you thank you thank you to my partner-in-crime/best-friend/wife/get-away-driver/culinary-ninja/dog-mom/cat-mom/plant-mom/garden-witch/friendly-misanthrope/bee Amanda. You are so unbelievably supportive and loving and wonderful. Thanks for sticking around.

Thank you Lisa, Scott, and Connor, and of course, thank you Mom and Dad.

Thank you to any of the musicians and artists mentioned in this book and so many others and to music and punk and poetry in general; If you didn't know, you are necessary and honestly saving people out there.

Additional thanks to Freeze Ray press for previously publishing "BtMI" in *Again I Wait Tor This To Pull Apart* (2015) and Into Quarterly for previously publishing "Open Your Ears and Breathe" in *Into Quarterly: Volume One: Austin* (2015).

I can't say thank you enough to anyone listed in the acknowledgments. Each of you has kept me going in some way.

Oh, and thank you Courtney for telling me to mention you and the rest of the crew in the book even though the thing was done before I met you assholes. So yeah, thanks.

Alright, y'all.

ABOUT THE AUTHOR

Kevin W. Burke was born and raised in the south suburbs of Chicago. After graduating from the University of Iowa, the former punk frontman moved to Austin, TX where he found a new home in the local poetry scene. I mean, the rest since then is kind of in this book, so yeah...

Aside from three DIY chapbooks, his work has previously been published by *Freeze Ray Press, Into Quarterly, Timber Mouse Publishing* (album), and *Button Poetry* (video). Burke is also the 2011 Austin Poetry Slam Champ, 2011 Southwest Shootout Slam Champ, and a two time Texas Grand Slam Poetry Festival Champion.

Kevin works as a firefighter, and he currently lives just south of Austin with his wonderfully supportive wife, their three almost equally supportive dogs, and a cat who doesn't give a shit either way, but in theory, loves them or whatever I guess.

www.kevinwburkepoetry.com

OTHER BOOKS BY TIMBER MOUSE AND WRITE ABOUT NOW

And Then Came The Flood — Lacey Roop
Love Letters to Balled Fists — Ebony Stewart
Universe in the Key of Matryoshka — Ronnie K. Stephens
Fat Girl Finishing School — Rachel Wiley
Rebel Hearts and Restless Ghosts — William James
They Rewrote Themselves Legendary — Ronnie K. Stephens
Home. Girl. Hood. — Ebony Stewart

www.ingramcontent.com/pod-product-compliance
Lightning Source LLC
Chambersburg PA
CBHW030447300426
44112CB00009B/1198